Monsters
and Mythical Creatures

Water
Monsters

Gail B. Stewart

ReferencePoint
Press®

San Diego, CA

ReferencePoint Press®

© 2011 ReferencePoint Press, Inc.
Printed in the United States

For more information, contact:
ReferencePoint Press, Inc.
PO Box 27779
San Diego, CA 92198
www.ReferencePointPress.com

LIBRARY OF CONGRESS CATALOGING-IN-PUBLICATION DATA

Stewart, Gail B. (Gail Barbara), 1949–
  Water monsters / by Gail B. Stewart.
    p. cm. — (Monsters and mythical creatures series)
  Includes bibliographical references and index.
  ISBN-13: 978-1-60152-136-1 (hardback)
  ISBN-10: 1-60152-136-7 (hardback)
  1. Sea monsters. I. Title.
  GR910.S74 2011
  398.24'54—dc22
                                                                2010026449

Contents

Introduction

Monsters Among Us?

group of friends was picnicking on the banks of the Buffeljags River in South Africa in January 2008 when one of the men, Daniel Cupido, heard a strange noise. It sounded, he said, like someone "bashing [into] a wall."[1] He went to investigate, following the sound to a low bridge. What he saw astonished him.

He described the creature to a South African newspaper as half fish, half woman, with white skin and long black hair. He said she was thrashing in the water. He thought she must be in trouble and was about to rush in to save her, when he noticed a red glow in her eyes—a sight that sent shivers down his spine. Even though he was frightened, he said he was pulled forward toward the fish-woman as though he were hypnotized. Cupido called out to his friends to come quickly, and that seemed to break the trance. They too had witnessed the half-human, half-fish creature.

Known as mermaids in the United States, these creatures are called Kaaimans in South Africa. They are considered to be very dangerous, for they are believed to drown humans by luring them into deep water. Cupido's mother, Dina, was with the group that day, and she heard the Kaaiman's voice that lured her son toward the water. It was a sound she will never, ever forget—a mournful, sorrowful cry. Dina said later, "My heart could take it no more."[2]

A Monster in Loch Ness?

Six thousand miles (9,656km) to the north, in 1965, a Scot named Ian Cameron was fishing for trout with a friend on Loch (Lake) Ness, when he saw something he had never seen before. He describes it today as "a large, black object—a whale-like object"[3] that broke the surface of the lake and then dove down deep again. He quickly called to his friend to come over to his end of the boat, and his friend saw the creature, too. Fascinated, the two watched it until they could see it no longer.

Reports of a monster of unknown origin in Scotland's Loch Ness date back centuries and continue today. Although scientific evidence is elusive, depictions such as this one suggest a resemblance to a prehistoric marine reptile species known as a plesiosaur.

Cameron, now a retired police supervisor in Scotland, says he understands why people would be skeptical of his story: "In no way am I even attempting to convert anybody to the religion of the object of Loch Ness. I mean, they can believe it, but it doesn't upset me if they don't believe it. Because I would question very much if I hadn't the extraordinary experience of *seeing* this object. If I hadn't seen it, I would have without question given a lot of skepticism to what it was."[4]

A Monster and Bad Luck

More than 50 years before, during the First World War in 1917, another strange sighting took place. An armed British ship called the *Hilary* was patrolling off the coast of Iceland, looking for German submarines. At about 9 A.M. on a sunny morning, Commander F.W. Dean was called to the bridge and told there was a strange object ahead. As he looked through his telescope, Dean saw that it was a huge cow-like creature, which he later described in his ship's log: "The head was about the shape of, but somewhat larger than . . . a cow, though with no observable protrusions such as horns or ears, and was black, except for the front of the face, which could be clearly seen to have a strip of whitish flesh, very like a cow has, between its nostrils."[5]

The creature raised its head several times to stare at the ship, and then Dean ordered his crew to fire on it with the ship's guns. After one of the shots hit the creature, it thrashed around and then went quiet. The ship's officer was very worried, feeling that it was bad luck to kill it. "We shall never reach port again,"[6] he told the crew. Interestingly, the *Hilary* was sunk three days later by a German submarine in the same place where the monster had been. The crew was rescued before the ship sank.

> # Did You Know?
> In 1812 the world's leading scientists declared the end of the age of zoological discovery, believing no new species of animals would ever be found.

A Different Kind of Science

Stories like these sound more like science fiction than fact. However, tens of thousands of such stories are told by people who have witnessed strange creatures in lakes, oceans, and rivers throughout the world. Some of the creatures are quite famous, such as the Loch Ness monster. Others, such as the Man-Eating Giant Catfish reputed to live below the lake Decatur dam in Decatur, Illinois, are less well known. Local legend claims that those monster catfish are the size of cows and may weigh up to 350 pounds (159kg) and measure more than 8 feet (2.4m) long.

While skeptics may be quick to dismiss stories about sea and lake monsters as foolish, some people are more willing to listen to the eyewitness accounts. These individuals are known as cryptozoologists—meaning that they study hidden or undocumented animals, known as "cryptids." The cryptid may be an animal originally thought to be merely legendary, but which someone claims to have witnessed. It also might be an animal that was assumed to have become extinct, which is one of the theories about the Loch Ness monster. The cryptid could also be a species that is known but, like

Tales of a giant, man-eating catfish in the Mississippi River may seem farfetched to some but not, perhaps, to the fishermen who hauled in this 646-pound (293kg) catfish from the Mekong River in northern Thailand.

the monster catfish, is far larger than any ever seen before. Or it may be an animal that has simply been hidden so long that scientists have never had an opportunity to document and classify it.

Cryptozoologists are scientists—usually biologists or zoologists who specialize in studying evidence of cryptids. As all scientists do, those who specialize in studying cryptids gather as much information as possible so they can better understand these creatures. This information may be in the form of photographs, video, or witness interviews. If they get lucky, they might even have some physical evidence to study, such as a footprint or a carcass washed up on shore.

Not So Crazy

Crazy as some of these stories may seem, cryptozoologists have good reason to study such creatures—especially those that live in water. Scientists know that they have not seen or catalogued all animal species on the planet. Frederick Grassle, the director of Rutgers University's Institute of Marine and Coastal Sciences, is an expert on water animals. He believes that Earth's oceans may contain millions of undiscovered animal species.

Cryptozoologists say that the people who live in an area are usually aware of new animals long before scientists finally see them. These scientists hope to find eyewitnesses to some of the cryptids they are researching. After all, people have reported the existence of strange water monsters—some of them terrifying—since ancient times.

Chapter 1

From the Ocean's Depths

Stories of monsters that inhabit the oceans have been told since the time of the earliest human civilizations. Most of these stories involve huge, serpentlike creatures that attacked not only the animals that lived in the sea but any humans who came too close.

The Scylla

One of the earliest stories about a sea serpent is found in *The Odyssey*, an epic tale written by the Greek poet Homer near the end of the eighth century B.C. The hero of the poem, Odysseus, is trying very hard to return home to his wife and son after fighting in the Trojan War. Along the way he has many terrifying adventures, including encounters with frightening sea monsters.

One of these, the Scylla, is unlike any creature Odysseus had ever encountered. Homer describes the fearsome creature this way:

> Inside [her cave] Scylla sits and yelps with a voice that you might take to be that of a young hound, but in truth she is a dreadful monster and no one—not even a god—could face her without being terror-struck. She has twelve misshapen feet, and six necks of the most prodigious length; and at the end of each neck she has a frightful head with three rows of teeth in each, all set very close together, so that they would crunch anyone to death in a moment, and she sits deep within her

shady cell thrusting out her heads and peering all round the rock, fishing for dolphins or dogfish or any larger monster that she can catch, of the thousands with which . . . [the sea] teems. No ship ever yet got past her without losing some men, for she shoots out all her heads at once, and carries off a man in each mouth.[7]

"The Most Sickening Sight"

Though the Scylla sounded terrifying, Odysseus preferred to take his chances with her rather than with Charybdis, the other sea monster that lived in the narrow shallows between Italy and Sicily. Charybdis was not scary to look at but was far more dangerous than the Scylla. Three times each day, Charybdis would drink and then vomit the entire sea, causing horrible tides and whirlpools that could sink the sturdiest ships.

Realizing it would be better to lose six of his men to the Scylla's six gaping mouths rather than the entire ship, Odysseus sailed far from Charybdis, closer to the Scylla. The result, he recalls in the

Odysseus braved the snapping jaws of the multi-headed sea monster Scylla (pictured) rather than chance losing his entire ship to Charybdis, a sea monster whose thrice-daily habit of drinking and vomiting the entire sea resulted in the sinking of many ships.

epic, was as painful as he had anticipated—each of Scylla's mouths snatched one of his men from the ship as he watched helplessly.

Scylla pounced down suddenly upon us and snatched up my six best men. I was looking at once after both ship and men, and in a moment I saw their hands and feet ever so high above me, struggling in the air as Scylla was carrying them off, and I heard them call out my name in one last despairing cry. As a fisherman, seated, spear in hand, upon some jutting rock throws bait into the water to deceive the poor little fishes, and spears them with the ox's horn with which his spear is shod, throwing them gasping on to the land as he catches them one by one—even so did Scylla land these panting creatures on her rock and munch them up at the mouth of her den, while they screamed and stretched out their hands to me in their mortal agony. This was the most sickening sight that I saw throughout all my voyages.[8]

A 350-Mile-Long Monster

Another sea serpent from ancient times is the Labbu, described as a massive sea serpent with wings and legs but living under the waves like a fish. It was said to be an astonishing 350 miles (563km) long and over 7 miles (11km) high. The size of the Labbu was measured as 50 "double hours" (a double hour being 7 miles (11km), or twice the distance a human could walk in one hour.)

> **Did You Know?**
>
> The International Society of Cryptozoology was founded in 1982 at the Smithsonian Institution in Washington, D.C.

An ancient Babylonian poem, found on now-ruined stone tablets from 3000 B.C., recounts how people all over the earth feared the Labbu. It was killing not only fish and sea animals but was snatching the birds from the air, crawling onto the land, and chasing down human prey. Knowing that no human was capable of killing such a gigantic creature, people begged the gods for a solution. The ancient poem explains that the gods were just as uncertain, knowing that

A Sea Monster in the Desert

In June 2010, scientists at the Natural History Museum in Paris announced that they had recovered the fossilized remains of an extraordinary whale. In the Pisco-Itca desert on the south coast of Peru, an area that was underwater millions of years ago, fossil hunters found a large fragment of the whale's lower jaw with teeth and large segments of its skull. Scientists estimate that it lived 12 million to 13 million years ago.

Though experts do not believe that the whale was larger than the sperm whales of today, there is no doubt that it was far more powerful than any known sea creature. Its teeth, an astonishing 14 inches (36cm) long, are twice the length of the prehistoric Megalodon shark, whose teeth were 7 inches (17.7cm) long.

"This was probably one of the most powerful predators ever found," said Olivier Lambert, the scientist who led the study. "I don't think such large teeth have ever been found before." The prehistoric creature was given the scientific name *Leviathan melvillei*—"Leviathan" after the enormous sea monster of the Bible and "melvillei" after Herman Melville, who wrote the classic *Moby-Dick*.

Quoted in Ian Sample, "Fossil Sperm Whale with Huge Teeth Found in Peruvian Desert," *Guardian*, June 30, 2010. www.guardian.co.uk.

it would be close to impossible for any of them to kill it, too. They asked one another, "Who will go and [slay] the *Labbu*?"[9]

As it turned out, one of them did, although his name has been lost in the crumbling tablets. The brave god "shot off [an arrow] and slew the *labbu* . . ." and the monster contained so much blood, "for three years [and] three months, one day and a [night] the blood of the *labbu* flowed."[10]

Sea Serpents Abound

Accounts of sea serpents are not limited to ancient poetry and legends. Hundreds of sightings of sea monsters have been reported throughout the world over the past five centuries. Some of the first accounts of such sightings in the Northern Hemisphere were gathered by Sweden's Archbishop Olaus Magnus in 1555.

One of the monsters he writes about had been spotted along the rocky coast of Bergen, in western Norway. The monster is described as over 200 feet (61m) long and 20 feet (6m) wide. Witnesses say the monster feasted on both fish and land animals:

Those who sail up along the coast of Norway to trade or to fish, all tell the remarkable story of how a serpent of fearsome size, 200 feet long and 20 feet wide, resides in rifts and caves outside Bergen. On bright summer nights this serpent leaves the caves to eat calves, lambs and pigs, or it fares out to the sea and feeds on sea nettles, crabs and similar marine animals. It has . . . long hair hanging from its neck, sharp black scales and flaming red eyes. It attacks vessels, grabs and swallows people, as it lifts itself up like a column from the water.[11]

Standing in a Sea Monster's Nostril

Many people also reported that they had happened upon a sea monster that was dying or already dead on the shore, enabling them to get a close-up view. A nineteenth-century article in the *Granby* (Quebec) *Mail* recounts just such a sighting—first reported three centuries earlier. Records from that

time indicate that a monstrous, fishlike creature washed up along the coast of Broadstairs in southeast England on July 9, 1574. According to the *Mail*, reports at the time said "the monster died the next day for the want of water, amid hideous roars that could be heard over a mile around."[12]

Albert Koch's Hoax

Albert Koch, a German collector of natural curiosities put on a sea monster exhibit in New York in 1845. The exhibit consisted of a complete skeleton of a prehistoric creature that Koch claimed to have found buried in Clarksville, Alabama. Though Clarksville is not on the Alabama coast, Koch explained the skeleton's presence by saying that the remains had been encased in "a stratum of yellowish lime rock . . . thrown to the surface by volcanic action."

The skeleton was 114 feet (34.7m) long. Koch gave it a Latin scientific name, *Hydrarchos sillimani*, after Benjamin Silliman, a Yale University professor who in 1827 had expressed his belief in the existence of sea monsters. Koch's sea monster did nothing to validate Silliman's beliefs. A Harvard professor of anatomy examined the skeleton and found it had been fashioned out of at least five different animals—most of them whales.

Quoted in Richard Ellis, *Monsters of the Sea*. New York: Alfred A. Knopf, 1994, p. 55.

Any suggestion that the monster was a whale seemed absurd to coastal residents, who were familiar with whales. No whale that they had ever seen could roar, as this beast did, and its size seemed well beyond any known whales of the time. According to the news account, "Some of the ribs were 14 feet long, the tongue was 15 feet, and whereas one man managed to creep into a nostril, three were able to stand erect in the monster's mouth, which opened 12 feet wide. The liver, when removed, made two cartloads and a six-horse team proved unequal to the effort of drawing one of the eyes along."[13]

The Gloucester Serpent

The eighteenth and nineteenth centuries brought a large number of sightings as ship traffic increased in the North Sea and the Atlantic between Europe and North America. One of the most exciting sightings occurred in the United States during the summer of 1817 in the harbor of Gloucester, Massachusetts—located just north of Boston.

On August 2 of that year, a one-page news report published in Boston announced that the largest sea monster ever seen in America had been witnessed by a large number of people:

> There was seen on Monday and Tuesday morning playing around the harbor between Eastern Point and Ten Pound Island, a SNAKE with his head and body about eight feet out of water, his head is in perfect shape as large as the head of a horse, his body is judged to be about FORTY-FIVE or FIFTY FEET IN LENGTH. . . . It was first seen by some fishermen ten or twelve days ago, but it was then generally believed to be a creature of the imagination. But he has since come within the harbor of Gloucester, and has been seen by hundreds of people.[14]

Massachusetts fishermen reported a giant snake-like sea monster frolicking near the Gloucester harbor in 1817. Much like this illustration, its horse-shaped head and a large portion of its serpent-shaped body could be seen well above the water line.

Other witnesses described it in a slightly different manner. One said its head was "much like the head of a turtle . . . and larger than the head on any dog" and noted that it had a large prong, or spike, coming out of its head. In addition, it had several humps along its back, which "resembled a string of buoys on a net."[15]

The sightings came to the attention of a local chapter of the prestigious Linnean Society, a London-based scientific organization that has been categorizing new species of plants and animals since it was founded in 1788. General David Humphries, a former member of George Washington's staff, was assigned the job of interviewing people who witnessed the Gloucester sea monster. The Linnean Society was impressed with the information and assigned the creature its own official Latin species name—*Scoliophis atlanticus*, which means "Atlantic humped snake."

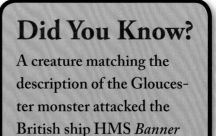

Did You Know?

A creature matching the description of the Gloucester monster attacked the British ship HMS *Banner* in April 1859.

"Their Observation Is . . . Without Merit"

While some people shared excitement in the Linnean Society's official recognition of the Gloucester sea serpent, others increasingly doubted the existence of such creatures. Skeptics pointed out that many so-called witnesses were illiterate or superstitious and that their accounts were suspect. In other cases, they said, bad weather or limited light might have clouded the vision of some witnesses, so they might not have known what they were seeing.

"The observers have no expert knowledge of zoology; their observation is, therefore, without merit," declared Sir Richard Owen, a prominent physician and scientist in nineteenth-century London. "A larger body of evidence from eye-witnesses might be got together in proof of ghosts than of the sea-serpent."[16]

Contrary to the belief of Owen and other skeptics, however, several sightings were reported by well-educated people. One example occurred on December 7, 1905, when two highly respected

British scientists witnessed what they believed to be a very large sea monster. Michael J. Nicoll and E.G.B. Meade-Waldo, fellows of the Zoological Society of London, were on a research cruise off the coast of Brazil. At 10:15 A.M., from the deck of their yacht *Valhalla*, Nicoll spotted a very large dorsal fin, which, he said, "resembled that of no fish I had previously seen."[17]

Meade-Waldo used his binoculars to track the fin as it cruised past them. He described it later as "dark seaweed-brown, somewhat crinkled at the edge."[18] The part of the fin he could see was nearly 6 feet (1.8m) long and between 18 inches (0.5m) and 24 inches (0.6m) high. As the two scientists watched, the creature's head rose out of the water. It was, they agreed, about the thickness of a thin man's body, and its head and neck were the same thickness. Meade-Waldo noted that it moved its head and neck back and forth in an odd manner. He recalled, too, that they were astonished at what they were seeing. "I will never forget Nicoll's face of amazement," he said, "when we looked at each other after we had passed out of sight of it."[19]

"This Is No Lie!"

Many people who have witnessed sea serpents have been reluctant to come forward, knowing they would be laughed at after telling what they had seen. Researcher W. Ritchie Benedict notes that as early as 1833, "passengers aboard steamers were swearing out statements, knowing full well they would be subject to ridicule."[20]

The Honorable James T. Brown, the chief justice of Saskatchewan's Kings Bench Court, recounted a story of a monster he saw off Victoria's coast while on vacation. "It was like a monstrous snake," he recalled. "It certainly wasn't any of those sea animals we know, like a porpoise, sea lion, and so on. I've seen them and know what they look like."[21]

Brown's wife and daughter were with him and corroborated his story. Brown was very reluctant to give a public account of the incident but did provide the following description of what the three

Sea Monsters and Submarines

Near the end of World War I, a British patrol boat sank a German submarine that had surfaced. The submarine's captain and crew abandoned the ship and were picked up by the British, who asked the crew why they had been cruising on the surface. The crew's story astonished them.

They had been on the surface the night before, recharging their batteries, with the hatch open. Then without warning a strange beast began climbing onto the sub. They described it as having small teeth, a horny sort of skull, and very large eyes. The creature was so large that the sub started tipping. Fearing that water would flood into the open hatch and sink them, the captain ordered his men to fire at the beast. "Every man on watch began firing a sidearm at the beast," the captain said. But it would not let go. Eventually it dropped back in the sea, but not before it damaged the plating on the forward deck. "That," the German captain told the British patrol, "is why you were able to catch us on the surface."

Quoted in "Sea Monster Tales." http://unmuseum.mus.pa.us.

of them saw: "His head, like a snake's, came out of the water four or five times and straight up. Six or seven feet from the head one of his big coils showed clearly. The coil itself was six or seven feet long, fully a foot thick, perfectly round and dark in color. There must have been a great length of him under water."[22]

However, Brown was so annoyed with the skeptical reaction he received, he made a sketch of the sea monster for the press and wrote, "This is no lie!"[23] at the bottom. He was quoted as saying, "A fellow goes out there [to Victoria on vacation] with a reputation rivaling that of George Washington and comes back as the biggest liar on the Pacific Coast."[24]

A Super-Otter?

Though sea monsters in most accounts have reptilian features, in some accounts they have mammal-like qualities. When World War II veteran Thomas Helm and his wife, Dorothy, took their boat for a ride in the Gulf of Mexico in March 1943, they never expected to encounter a sea monster, but that is exactly what happened. They were sailing along the northwest coast of Florida, when Helm saw what he thought was an otter swimming directly for their boat.

"The creature had a head the size of a basketball on a neck which reached four feet out of the water," Helm later wrote. "Staring for a brief moment in total disbelief, I quickly turned to attract Dorothy's attention, but immediately saw that she too saw the swimming creature." According to Helm, the creature stared back at them, then did a double take and dove down under the water. "The entire head and neck were covered with wet fur, which lay close to the body," he said. "The head of this creature . . . was that of a monstrous cat."[25] Though they searched the area, they never found it again.

> **Did You Know?**
>
> The Bible mentions a fire-breathing sea monster called Leviathan that, when angry, would use its breath to make the oceans boil.

Modern Sightings

Sightings of sea monsters have continued into modern times. In June 1999 Arnt Helge Molvaer saw a creature he estimated to be about 90 feet (27.5m) long swimming parallel to the shore in Aelesund, Norway. He watched it through binoculars for several minutes and then ran back to his house to get his video camera. He returned in less than an hour with his son, Per Tore, and the monster was still there. Molvaer's son said it reminded him of an anaconda (a tropical South American snake that can weigh up to 550 pounds (250kg) and can open its jaws wide enough to swallow a whole jaguar or small deer)—but much larger. The two watched the sea monster drag a whale carcass from the shore and begin to feed on it. The video Molvaer shot stirred public interest when it was shown on Norwegian television.

Sea monsters have been spotted in modern times within the Southern Hemisphere, too. A researcher of unexplained phenomena named Guillermo R. Gimenez reported in 2005 that a sea serpent had been spotted off the coast of Buenos Aires, Argentina, several times since 1994. Nicknamed "Joselito" by locals, it was described as being at least 32 feet (10m) to 39 feet (12m) long, with serrated fins—"like the dinosaurs they show us in books or magazines," said one witness, commercial fisherman Carlos Mino. Mino also said that he and his crew never felt as though they were in danger. "It appears to be a peaceful speci-

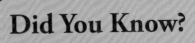

Did You Know?

A water monster nick-named Chessie is said to live in Chesapeake Bay, a massive estuary surrounded by Maryland and Virginia.

keptics suggest hat a sea monster ighting off the coast of Irgentina might have een a sea lion such s the one pictured here or some other sea reature. Witnesses eject that idea.

men. At no time did it threaten us," he recalled later, "and I could go as far to say that it ignored us."[26]

Others who have encountered Joselito reject the idea that they mistook a whale or sea lion or some other creature for a sea monster, says Gimenez. "We have seen whales, baby whales, sea lions, penguins and others species," insists one witness, "but we have never seen an animal with these characteristics."[27] Whatever monstrous creatures have been appearing throughout the world, they are not recognizable to those most familiar with the sea.

Chapter 2

Mer-People

Some of the oldest sea monster legends tell of bizarre half-human, half-fish creatures that can live both in the sea and on land. Historian Richard Carrington notes that mermaidlike beings appear in the legends and folklore of most every culture. "There is not an age, and hardly a country in the world," he writes, "whose folklore does not contain some reference to mermaids or mermaid-like creatures. They have been alleged to appear in a hundred different places, from the mist covered shores of Norway and Newfoundland to the palm-studded islands of the tropic seas."[28]

Remarkably, stories of mermaids or mermen go beyond folklore and legend. Accounts of people who claim to have seen or interacted with such beings date back centuries and, in some cases, only a year or two.

Early Accounts of Mer-People

The earliest accounts of mer-people (the word *mer* means "ocean" in Middle English) come from around 5000 B.C. in ancient Babylonia. The Babylonians worshipped a sea god named Oannes, who lived on land during the day, but returned to the sea each night. The Babylonians believed that Oannes had emerged from the Red Sea because he wanted to teach humans everything they needed to build a great civilization. The skills he was supposed to have taught these ancient people were farming methods, mathematics, and the ability to create a written alphabet.

Physically, Oannes looked different from the half-fish, half-human beings portrayed in most illustrations and sculptures. His body was that of a large fish, but on top of the fish head was a man's head. And beneath his fishy tail, Oannes had human legs—almost looking like a man wearing a fish costume.

Oannes had a female counterpart, the goddess Atargatis. She resembled the more common version of a mermaid—a woman from the waist up, and a fish from the waist down. Like Oannes, Atargatis was kind to humans, providing them with a set of rules for being kind and gracious to one another, as well as the ability to study the stars to predict the future.

Triton the Enforcer

The ancient Greeks had their own ideas of mer-people, which were quite different from those of the Middle East. Triton was the son of Poseidon, the powerful god of the seas, and was Poseidon's messenger. Ancient sculptors and artists depicted Triton as a merman, with the torso and head of a man and the lower body of a fish. His shoulders were said to be layered with shells and barnacles, and he carried a conch shell everywhere.

Ancient mariners returned from their voyages with tales of mermen and mermaids, sometimes also called tritons. This sixteenth-century painting depicts an encounter between the half human–half fish creatures and Italian explorer Amerigo Vespucci as he made his way to the New World.

But unlike Oannes and Atargatis, Triton was not usually a kind or helpful god. He was an enforcer, who carried out punishments against humans who had displeased Poseidon. Triton would blow on his huge conch shell, and the sound would stir up the waves and cause storms, driving the unlucky human traveling in a ship to either veer wildly off course or be killed as his boat crashed against the rocks.

In later Greek myths, mermen were often called tritons. In the second century B.C., a Greek traveler named Pausanias visited Rome and claimed that these tritons were no mere myths, for he had seen one of these creatures with his own eyes. As Pausanias describes the tritons:

> On their heads they have hair which resembles the hair of marsh frogs both in hue and in this, that you cannot separate one hair from another. The rest of their body bristles with fine scales like those of a shark. They have gills under their ears and a human nose, but their mouth is wider, and their teeth are those of a beast. Their eyes, I think, are blue, and they have hands, fingers, and nails like the shells of mussels. Under their breast and belly, instead of feet, they have a tail like a dolphin's.[29]

Sirens on the Rocks

Mermaids, too, were a part of Greek mythology. They were called Sirens, and at first they were described as a combination of beautiful women and birds. In later stories, however, they were described as having the upper body of a woman and the lower body of a fish. But no matter what they looked like, the Sirens were always bad news for sailors.

Sirens often sunned on the rocks near the shallows of the ocean and sang, hoping to lure sailors with their music. Their songs were

A Strategy for Avoiding the Sirens

Odysseus, in Homer's *The Odyssey*, was so curious to hear the music of the Sirens, he told his men to tie him to the mast as they approached the rocks where they sang. He also insisted that the sailors plug their own ears with beeswax, so they would not be affected. When he heard the song, Homer says, Odysseus shouted at his men, ordering them to release him. However, they only bound him more tightly, so he could not fling himself into the water. When they had passed safely away, Odysseus frowned at his men, so they knew he could no longer hear the deadly Sirens, and they continued on their journey.

so beautiful and their voices so haunting that sailors would be drawn toward them like magnets. Even the most experienced sailors fell under the Sirens' spell, hypnotized so completely that they would step right off the deck of a ship into the water or would steer the boat purposely onto the jagged rocks where the Sirens lay— just to get closer to that lovely music. Once in the clutches of the Sirens, the seamen were lost forever—imprisoned in the creatures' underwater kingdom. It is little wonder that seagoing men greatly feared the irresistible Sirens.

The Mermaid of the Biloxi Indians

It was not only sailors who had reason to fear mer-people. If one often-told story is true, one mermaid may have been responsible for the mass extinction of an entire Native American tribe called the Pascagoula—often known as the Biloxi Indians. Until 1539 the Biloxi lived along the Pascagoula River between New Orleans and Biloxi, Mississippi.

They were a peaceful people. They loved and honored the river mermaid and kept a statue of her in a small temple in their village. Each evening they gathered to worship her along the riverbank and

Mermaids frolic in the waves in this hand-colored woodcut. Mermaidlike creatures can be found in the legends of cultures worldwide.

listen to her song rising from the deep, dark water. The music was so sweet, writes researcher E. Randall Floyd, "brave warriors would weep under its spell."[30]

Whether or not the mermaid part of the story is true, says Floyd, "the fact is that the Biloxi Indians did suddenly and inexplicably vanish during the early sixteenth century, only weeks after a white-bearded priest had appeared to them with a crucifix in hand, demanding that they abandon their superstitious belief in an underwater goddess."[31]

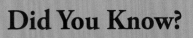

According to the legend, the priest convinced the Biloxi that their belief in the mermaid was foolish and that his Christian religion was far more powerful. Eventually he persuaded the tribe to dismantle their temple and throw the statue into the river. When the mermaid realized what had happened, however, she rose out of the deep water and called to her people to leap into the river to join her in paradise:

> Come to me, come to me, children of the sea,
> Neither bell, book, nor cross shall win ye from your Queen.[32]

The Biloxi realized that they had made a mistake by abandoning the mermaid. Joining hands, every man, woman, and child leaped from the bank into the water. From that time onward, there has been no sign of any member of the Biloxi. For some unknown reason, however, the river still sings. Notes one reporter from the *Meridian* [Mississippi] *Star*, the lower Pascagoula River "emits a low, mournful humming or singing in certain areas. These sounds have been heard for generations by many who have visited the river, and are still heard today."[33]

"In the Face They Look Like Men"

Human encounters with mermen and mermaids have gone beyond myths and legends. Actual accounts of human interaction with mer-people cannot be confirmed, but they are abundant. Interestingly, the eyewitness descriptions of the creatures differ greatly.

Most have reported that mermaids are very beautiful and often mention their long, flowing hair. However, Christopher Columbus was not impressed with their appearance on January 9, 1493, as he sailed back to Spain after his first transatlantic voyage. In his journal he writes that he saw three mermaids who "came out of the water, but were not as pretty as they are depicted, for somehow in the face they look like men."[34]

The explorer Henry Hudson, sailing in the Arctic Ocean more than a century later, in 1608, describes the mermaid he and his crew saw in quite a different way:

This morning, one of our companie looking over boord saw a Mermaid, and calling up some of the companie to see her, one more came up, and by the time shee was come close to the ship's side, looking earnestly on the men: a little after, a Sea [wave] came and overturned her. From the Navill [navel] upward, her backe and breasts were like a woman's (as they say that saw her) her body as big as one of us; her skin very white; and long haire hanging down of colour blacke; in her going down, they saw her tayle, which was like the tayle of a Porpesse.[35]

And years later, in 1632, witnesses reported seeing a mermaid swimming toward the Chilean shore. They said she was "of pleasing appearance, with long, loose, blond hair or mane; she carried a child in her arms. And when she dived, they saw that she had a tail and back of a fish, covered with thick scales, like little shells."[36]

Mermaids Up Close

Few eyewitness accounts are as fascinating as those in which people have actually interacted with mermaids (not usually mermen, for they are thought to be uninterested in humans). For example, in 1833 three fishermen testified before a local magistrate that they had caught a mermaid about 30 miles (48km) off the coast of Yell, one of the northern islands of Scotland. They reported that the mermaid was about three feet (1m) long and had small hands with webbed fingers. Its eyes were blue, and its head tapered to a point on top. The mermaid had neither ears nor chin. The fishermen said that when they pulled it onto the boat it made pitiful moaning noises, so they threw it back into the sea.

Some of the encounters with mermaids have not ended happily. For example, in 1830 a crowd of people who lived in the Outer Hebrides in Scotland saw a small mermaid swimming in the sea. They tried to catch it, but it swam away quickly until a boy threw a sharp rock that hit the mermaid in the back, killing it. A few days later the mermaid's body washed onto the shore.

People in the nearby village rushed to get a glimpse of the creature and commented on the whiteness of the skin and its long,

Help from a Merman

It was an unusual creature who, according to some Native American stories, was responsible for leading their forebears from their original home in Asia to North American shores. One day, when they were suffering in Asia from not having enough to eat, a merman took pity on them. He had green hair and a green beard, a face that was shaped like that of a porpoise, and a forked tail. According to historian S. Baring-Gould, the people were very frightened. "But if our people were frightened at seeing a man, riding upon the waves. . . . if our people were frightened at seeing a man who could live in the water like a fish or a duck, how much more were they frightened when they saw that from his breast down, he was actually a fish, or rather two fishes, for each of his legs was a whole and distinct fish." Following him, they safely arrived in North America.

Quoted in Gary Varner, *Creatures in the Mist: Little People, Wild Men, and Spirit Beings Around the World.* New York: Algora, 2007, p. 19.

dark hair. According to researcher George Eberhart, the mermaid "looked like a three- or four-year-old child with . . . a salmonlike tail, but without scales."[37] The villagers made a wooden coffin for the mermaid and buried it.

Mistaken Identity or Sideshow Hoaxes?

Eyewitness accounts may at times sound convincing, but few people in the twenty-first century actually believe that mer-people exist. More likely, experts say, is that people who thought they saw a mermaid or merman mistook some other creature for the half-human, half-fish beings. People who claim to have seen mermaids swimming in the sea or sitting on rocks may have actually seen seals or manatees. Because the manatee has a rounded head that looks a little more human than fishlike, it could possibly be mistaken for a human at a distance.

Hoaxes, too, could explain many reported mermaid sightings. Without a doubt, some have tried to cash in on people's fascination with mermaids. One of these was P.T. Barnum, the famous nineteenth-century showman and promoter. Barnum was always on the lookout for unusual and grotesque attractions to display in his American Museum in New York. He believed a mermaid would make him a lot of money so he bought a fake mermaid skeleton, which consisted of the cojoined top half of a small monkey and the dried-up bottom half of a fish. Barnum's mermaid attracted thousands of visitors. In his autobiography Barnum described it as being very different from attractive mermaids of literature and myth. It was, he wrote, an "ugly, dried-up, black-looking specimen about three feet long . . . that looked like it had died in great agony."[38]

Not Always Hoaxes or Mistaken Identity

But while seals, manatees, and hoaxes like Barnum's may explain many mermaid sightings, they cannot explain them all. In fact, some of the most recent mermaid stories have been the most convincing. In July 2000, for example, a woman and her daughter walking along the coast in southern Norway saw what appeared to both of them

to be a mermaid swimming very close to shore. Ilsa Tronson, age 33, says that she saw the tail of what looked like a green fish but then noticed that the fish had what appeared to be a human face and arms. Tronson and her daughter watched the mermaid dive in and out of the waves for about 30 seconds before it headed out to deeper water.

In 2004 an American college instructor named Michael Souza described his visit to the seaside city of Fukuoka, Japan, where he discovered a small shrine called the Mermaid Temple. The

From a distance, could people have mistaken the rounded face of a manatee (pictured) for the human head of a mermaid? This has been offered as one explanation for mermaid sightings.

legend behind the shrine is that mermaids have always lived in the waters off the coast of Japan, especially those waters that separate Japan from Korea. One day many years ago, fishermen had caught a mermaid in one of their nets by accident, and it died. They took it to this nearby shrine and placed its remains in a box, which has remained there for centuries. Many residents of the city, Souza learned, visit the shrine to view the mermaid's bones and still believe that mermaids live in the waters that separate Japan from Korea.

While visiting the temple one day, Souza met a man named Saburo Nakamura, who said he had worked on fishing boats when he was a young man. On several occasions, said Nakamura, he saw mermaids. On one occasion, a mermaid had gotten tangled in a fishing net, just like the mermaid in the legend. This mermaid also died—in this case, because the fishermen were too afraid to go near it to cut it loose.

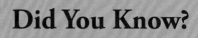

Did You Know?

The sound of Triton's conch was said to have been so loud that it frightened even the giants that roamed the earth in those days.

No Chance of Being Mistaken

Souza asked Nakamura if he thought it possible that he was mistaken—that maybe the "mermaid" was not a mermaid at all but rather a large, deformed fish of some sort:

> He looked a little taken aback and said "No." He told me how his family had grown up on the water. Many years ago, Fukuoka had been a small fishing community where people knew all the varieties of fish and sea life in the waters off their town. He acted . . . slighted, as if I had insulted him a bit, and asked me, "Could you confuse a rabbit and a dog at two meters on a clear day?"[39]

For someone not well acquainted with fish and marine life, such a mistake might be easy to make. This was not the case for Nakamura, who had lived near the sea his whole life. He provided detailed descriptions of the mermaids: Their faces were not pretty, he told Souza, but rather more like the faces of sheep. Their bodies were about the size of a small person—about 3 feet 6 inches (107cm) tall—and had very human-looking hands.

A Million-Dollar Mermaid?

Reports of sightings of mer-people are less common today than they once were, but they do happen. In August 2009 an Israeli newspaper reported that numerous people had seen a mermaid near Kiryat Yam, a suburb of Haifa, Israel. Shlomo Cohen, a soldier, says he was with a group of people who were the first to report it: "I was with friends when suddenly we saw a woman laying on the sand in a weird way. At first I thought she was just another sunbather but when we approached, she jumped into the water and disappeared. We were all in shock because we saw she had a tail. At least five of us saw it and we all couldn't believe it."[40]

Others reported seeing the mermaid swimming, diving, and turning flips in the water near the beach. They have described the creature as a cross between a little girl and a dolphin. Israeli authorities announced that they would pay a cash prize for the first person to provide a video or photograph that proved the existence of the mermaid. As of April 2010 no one had claimed the prize. It seems that mermaids (and mermen, for that matter) are as elusive in the twenty-first century as they have been throughout history.

Chapter 3

The Monster in Loch Ness

Some of the most well-known water monsters are not found in oceans but in freshwater rivers or lakes. The most famous sea monster in the world is found in Loch (the Scottish word for "lake") Ness in Scotland. Photos and video footage of the monster, as well as eyewitness testimonials, have intrigued people from all over the world, making Loch Ness a popular place for tourists hoping to catch a glimpse.

A Strange Sort of Loch

Loch Ness is no ordinary lake. It is long and stringy—more like a 24-mile-long river (38.6km). However, the lake makes up in depth what it lacks in width. Scientists estimate that it is likely 1,000 feet (305m) deep in some places—which is more than 100 feet (30.5m) deeper than the deepest part of Lake Michigan. At that great depth, some experts say, the lake could easily provide a suitable habitat (or hiding place) for a large water monster. No one actually knows if such a creature exists, though people have tried for years to come up with definitive proof that "Nessie," as the monster is known, is real. While definitive proof is in short supply, eyewitnesses who swear that they have seen Nessie are plentiful.

An Ancient Monster?

Though most of the sightings of the Loch Ness monster have occurred since 1933, one interesting story comes from around the sixth century A.D. The story involves an Irish holy man known as St. Columba. While traveling in Scotland in the year 565 he came to the River Ness, which flows into the lake, and there he saw some people burying a man. The man apparently had died after an attack by a large monster that lived in the River Ness.

The threat of such a beast did not deter St. Columba; he directed one of his companions to swim across the river to fetch a boat. As the man began swimming, the monster attacked. St. Columba's biographer, Adomnam, later wrote: "The monster, which, so far from being satiated, was only roused for more prey, was lying at the bottom of the stream, and when it felt the water disturbed above by the man swimming, suddenly rushed out, and, giving an awful roar, darted after him, with its mouth wide open, as the man swam in the middle of the stream."[41]

St. Columba reacted quickly, with startling results, according to Adomnam: "Then the blessed man observing this, raised his holy

Scotland's Loch Ness on a beautiful, sunny day offers no sense of the long-running mystery that lies beneath the water's surface. Accounts of an elusive monster living in the lake are intriguing but so far unproven.

hand, while all the rest, brethren as well as strangers, were stupefied with terror, and, invoking the name of God, formed the saving sign of the cross in the air, and commanded the ferocious monster, saying, 'Thou shalt go no further, nor touch the man; go back with all speed.'"[42]

According to the story, these instructions were all it took. The monster was so terrified of St. Columba that, says Adomnam, it "fled more quickly than if it had been pulled back with ropes."[43]

Fast Forwarding to the Twentieth Century

Over the years, a few sightings of odd-looking creatures in and around Loch Ness and the nearby rivers were reported, but with no specific details. For example, a man named Mackenzie reported what he thought was an animal of some kind in the middle of the lake in 1871 or 1872. According to his statement, the creature "seemed to me to look exactly like an upturned boat, and went at great speed, wriggling and churning up the water."[44]

But it was not until 1933 that a flurry of reports of a mysterious creature in Loch Ness began to surface. The timing for these sightings is no coincidence, say experts. Just weeks before the reports began to come in, an old road running around the north end of the lake was expanded, using great amounts of dynamite to blast through stone and rock.

The goal of the renovation was to provide people the opportunity to see views of the lake from the road. Many believe that the creature or creatures might have been in the lake for years or even centuries but were too difficult to see prior to the roadwork. "My view is that Nessie could have been swimming around in Loch Ness for years, but no one could have seen it," says Dolores Ann Griffith, a Chicago resident who has visited the Loch Ness area four times in the hope of catching a glimpse of the monster. "It's too bad, because if this road

A Secret Passage?

One theory as to why the monster of Loch Ness is so difficult to pin down has to do with the shape and depth of the lake itself. The lake lies within a narrow valley that straddles a deep crack in the Earth's surface, called a fault. Of all the lakes within the valley, Loch Ness is the deepest. Some scientists have suggested that a fissure may exist within the lake, providing a passageway between the lake and the ocean. This idea fits with speculation that Nessie might be descended from a prehistoric creature that, over time, has grown adept at living in both freshwater and saltwater environments but spends much of its time in the ocean.

had been there in years past, who knows how many more witnesses there would be, and how much more information we would have about Nessie?"[45]

Eyewitness Accounts of Nessie

Whatever the reason for the rash of these twentieth-century sightings, the first of them occurred at about 3 P.M. on April 13, 1933. John Mackay and his wife were driving near the loch when they stopped the car to observe a creature they described as "an enormous animal rolling and plunging."[46] The creature was about 100 yards (91m) from shore.

Mrs. Mackay said that she and her husband saw a large wake, much like a good-sized boat would create as it moved through the water, and two black humps moving in a line. At first, she explained, she thought the animal was a whale, because of the bluish black color. Also, it moved in a manner similar to whales she had seen—a sort of rising and sinking in a wavelike pattern.

Within a month of the newspaper article about the event, 20 more eyewitnesses came forward with their own stories. George

Spicer and his wife reported one of the most interesting of these stories on July 22. When they saw the creature, it was not in the water at all but moving across the road about 50 yards (45.7m) in front of their car.

According to one source, Spicer described it as being at least 25 feet (7.6m) long and a grayish color "like a dirty elephant or rhinoceros."[47] Another source recounts Spicer's description of the encounter in more detail: "Although I accelerated quickly towards it, it had disappeared into the Loch by the time I reached the spot. There was no sign of it in the water. I am a temperate man, but I am willing to take any oath that we saw this Loch Ness beast. I am certain that this creature was of a prehistoric species."[48]

What Sort of Monster?

Since the Spicer sightings, tens of thousands of people have descended on the Loch Ness area, hoping to see the monster for themselves. Most have left disappointed, but more than 3,000 people swear that they have seen Nessie—even if just for a few seconds. As a result of these sightings, cryptozoologists and other scientists have studied the testimonies of the witnesses in an effort to classify the monster by its physical characteristics.

> **Did You Know?**
>
> Hoping to prove Nessie's existence, the promoter of a June 2007 rock concert held on the shores of Loch Ness handed out 33,000 free cameras to concertgoers in the hope that someone would get a shot of the monster. No one did.

One idea about the monster's identity is based on the description of the Spicers and others who described it as a prehistoric-looking animal, such as a dinosaur. Some experts suggest that Nessie might belong to a class of reptiles known as plesiosaurs. They thrived on Earth more than 200 million years ago and are believed to have gone extinct 65 million years ago, at the same time as the dinosaurs.

The prehistoric plesiosaur had a barrel-shaped body, flippers, and a long, slender neck and small head. These features also fit descriptions of the Loch Ness monster, depicted here in computer artwork.

Beatrix Potter's Ideas About Nessie

English children's author Beatrix Potter, best known for her Peter Rabbit and Mrs. Tiggy-Winkle books, had a strong interest in sea monsters. Potter wrote a letter in 1934 to researcher Rupert Gould, who had just completed a book on the Loch Ness monster. She had some ideas she wanted to share. "May I hazard a suggestion about the humps?" she wrote.

> These beasts—whatever they are—frequent deep waters. They are able to sustain immense variations of pressure. I suggest that the humps may result from a power of self inflation under a very elastic skin for the purpose of equalising pressure. Frogs & toads, especially the latter, have power of inflation. Toads let off acrid water. Their inflation is in the belly. But it is conceivable that this beast may have a very loose elastic skin all round its body.

Quoted in StrangeArk.com, "Beatrix Potter on the Loch Ness Monster," November 26, 2006. www.strangeark.com.

But if Nessie was a plesiosaur, it would fit the profile—anywhere from 8 feet (2.4m) to 60 feet (18m) long, with a barrel-shaped body and flippers instead of legs. Plesiosaurs had long, slender necks and small heads, too. One nineteenth-century dinosaur scholar described a plesiosaur as being "like a snake threaded through the body of a turtle."[49]

Another idea, suggested by zoologist Maurice Burton, is that Nessie could be related not to dinosaurs but to eels. Like eels, Nessie seems to spend more time submerged than atop the water, and, according to some reports, it comes out of the water to move around on the land. However, since lake eels are generally no longer than

24 inches (60cm) said Burton, it would have to be "one of greater proportion than any known to science."[50]

"Nessie Fever"

Whatever its biological classification, Nessie has remained a hot topic. "You can't go anywhere in Scotland without people talking about [the monster]," says amateur cryptozoologist Madeline Mathes, who has visited the area several times from her native New Zealand. "They call it 'Nessie fever'—it's almost like people's fascination with a movie star. I was there in the 1950s with my parents, and just visited most recently in October of 2009. The first question people always ask me when I return is 'Did you see Nessie?'"[51]

However, Nessie's fame has a downside. Some people want to profit from the witnesses' stories of their sightings. Circuses and museums put bounties on the monster, offering tens of thousands of dollars to anyone who can capture it live or produce its carcass.

In late 1933 the *London Daily Mail* hired a big game hunter named Marmaduke Wetherell to track down the monster. The newspaper was confident that he could get results, but even his editors were astonished at how quickly he found evidence of Nessie. Walking along the shoreline of the lake, Wetherell came across fresh footprints of a very large, four-toed animal. He told the paper that by his estimations, the beast must be at least 20 feet (6m) long.

Did You Know?

Both the *Encyclopedia Britannica* and the Smithsonian Institution receive more requests for information on the Loch Ness monster than any other topic.

Wetherell made a plaster cast of the footprint and sent it to scientists at the world-famous British Museum in London. After analyzing it, scientists found that the print was that of a hippopotamus. Someone most likely made it by using a stuffed hippo's foot to create the print—much to the disappointment of the public, who hoped for a solid bit of proof that Nessie really existed. Not surprisingly, the embarrassed newspaper editors fired Wetherell immediately.

Hoaxes

Gerald McSorley shows off the fossilized vertebrae of a plesiosaur, which he found on the shores of Loch Ness in 2003. Experts say someone, though not necessarily McSorley, planted the fossil at that location.

Sea monster hoaxes are fairly common, but some sightings sound so authentic that hunters cannot let them pass without at least some investigation. For example, researchers were excited when they heard about a fossilized vertebrae found in the shallow waters of Loch Ness. In 2003 a retired scrap metal dealer named Gerald McSorley had fallen in the lake when he tripped over the bones, embedded in rock.

Excitement increased when the experts positively identified the vertebrae as those of a plesiosaur, the prehistoric reptile that resembled eyewitness descriptions of Nessie. However, an analysis of the rock in which the bones were embedded showed it was limestone—found in saltwater, not freshwater. Without a doubt, they concluded, the fossilized remains had been planted there—not necessarily by McSorley but by someone hoping to cause a stir when the bones were found.

Another burst of excitement occurred in 2005 when two American students visiting Scotland claimed they had found a huge tooth stuck in the carcass of a deer on the shore of Loch Ness. The students announced on a Web site that the tooth could very well belong to Nessie and claimed that although a game warden had confiscated the tooth, they had photos. However, it did not take scientists long to identify the object not as a tooth but as a piece of deer antler. The whole event turned out to be a publicity stunt for a soon-to-be-released horror novel about Loch Ness.

The Surgeon's Photograph

Of all the hoaxes over the years, the most disappointing to Loch Ness researchers was a photograph, submitted to the *London Daily Mail* in 1934 by a surgeon named R. Kenneth Wilson. It shows what appears to be the long neck and head of an unknown creature emerging from Loch Ness—very similar to the plesiosaur-like

The shadowy shape of a long-necked creature purported to be the Loch Ness monster can be seen in this photograph. "The Surgeon's Photograph," as it came to be known, created a stir among Nessie watchers when it appeared in the London Daily Mail *in 1934.*

monster that the Spicers and other witnesses described. And because Wilson had the reputation of being a very honest, truthful man, "the Surgeon's Photograph," as it became known, was thought to be real.

However, in 1994 Loch Ness monster researchers Alastair Boyd and David Martin demonstrated that the photo was a hoax. In their book *Nessie: The Surgeon's Photograph Exposed* Boyd and Martin explain that Ian Wetherell (son of Marmaduke Wetherell) had claimed in 1975 that Wilson's photo was a fake. Wetherell said that his father had faked the photograph by having him and his stepbrother fashion a tiny monster. To make it appear that the monster was rearing its head above the water, the boys put it atop a 14-inch (36cm) toy submarine, which was not visible in the photo.

Wetherell said his father did this out of revenge because the newspaper had fired him. To conceal the fact that he was behind the hoax, his father persuaded Wilson to have the photo developed and sell it to the newspaper. The news was disappointing to millions of people who had seen the photograph. "It was *the* definitive picture of Nessie for decades," says Mathes. "And all of a sudden—it was nothing at all."[52]

> ## Did You Know?
>
> In 1979 some researchers briefly considered bringing trained dolphins (that can survive for short times in freshwater) with cameras strapped to their backs into Loch Ness, to try to get an underwater image of Nessie.

"I Would Stake My Life on Their Existence"

Hoaxes are always disappointing, but they do not represent the final word on Nessie's existence. A few photographic images have withstood more rigorous examination. Respected Nessie researcher Tim Dinsdale was at the lake in April 1960 when he saw a "long oval shape, a distinct mahogany color . . . well above the water."[53] It was moving about 10 miles per hour (16kmh)—fast enough to leave a wake. As the object began moving, he realized that he could very well be looking at the back end of the monster as it moved through the water.

Dinsdale got about four minutes of the action on film before the object disappeared. Though skeptics insisted the shape was nothing more than a fishing boat, they were proved wrong. The film was analyzed by Britain's Joint Air Reconnaissance Intelligence Center, which analyzes satellite photographs and other surveillance imagery for Britain's armed forces. The center compared Dinsdale's film with footage of a boat moving in the same direction on the lake. After its review, the center stated that Dinsdale's footage was very probably "an animate object."[54]

Those who have witnessed the creature firsthand have no doubts about the monster's existence. Ironically, one of these witnesses is Boyd, one of the men who positively discredited the Surgeon's Photograph. In 1979 he and his wife experienced a sighting of what he believes is the monster:

> I am so convinced of the reality of these creatures that I would actually stake my life on their existence. I trust my eyesight . . . I used to make my living teaching people how to observe, and I know that the thing I saw was not a log or an otter or a wave, or anything like that. It was a large animal. It came heaving out of the water, something like a whale. I mean, the part that was actually on the surface when it stopped rolling through was at least 20 feet long. It was totally extraordinary. It's the most amazing thing I've ever seen in my life, and if I could afford to spend the rest of my life looking for another glimpse of it, I would.[55]

Chapter 4

Beasts in the Lakes

The Loch Ness monster is without a doubt the most famous lake monster, but it is not the only one. From mysterious cryptids that look like dinosaurs to gigantic versions of common animals, a number of other freshwater monsters are believed to reside in lakes around the world. For centuries the stories of these creatures have both frightened and fascinated nearby residents—some of whom have witnessed them firsthand.

Ogopogo

One of the most famous of these is the Ogopogo, a monster believed to live in Canada's Lake Okanagan in British Columbia. Ogopogo is not the creature's original name. Long before the first European settlers arrived in North America, it was called N'ha-a-itkh by the Shushwap Indians, who worshipped it as a water god.

The earliest descriptions of Ogopogo are pictographs found in caves near the lake. One shows a monster with the head of a horse, humps on its back, and a forked tail. Another shows a frightening monster with a gaping mouth and several humps on a long, snaky shape. The 750-foot depths (230m) of Lake Okanagan were perfect for the monster, which some have claimed was nearly 70 feet (21.3 m) long.

According to Shushwap legend, the monster was fearsome in more than its physical appearance. It usually stayed in its home under a little island near

Squally Point, a sharp bend in the lake's west side. When perturbed, however, it would swim out into the middle of the lake and create vicious windstorms and deadly whirlpools to sink boats and destroy camps on the shore.

Did You Know?

Section 26 of the British Columbia Fisheries Act makes it illegal for anyone to shoot or otherwise harm Ogopogo.

The Shushwap people were very mindful of the changeable nature of the creature's moods. They always painted their canoes with special symbols that they believed would please the monster. They also made sure to bring it a gift when they went out on the water. According to researcher Mary Moon, "No Indian in his right mind would venture out onto the lake without taking along a small pig, dog, or chicken as a sacrifice."[56]

One Shushwap story illustrates the consequences of not taking such precautions. An Indian named Timbasket refused to

Scotland's Loch Ness is not the world's only source of lake monster stories. Images of serpent-shaped water monsters rising from lakes, similar to the scene depicted here, appear in ancient pictographs found in caves near Lake Okanagan in western Canada.

paint his canoe with symbols or to throw an animal into the water to appease Ogopogo. With his family in the canoe, he even paddled close to the island where the monster was said to lurk. But just as Timbasket was gloating that he had no fear of the monster, it rose from its cave deep underwater and, with its tail, whipped the water into a huge storm. Timbasket and his family were never seen again.

The Monster Up Close

The sightings continued with the coming of European settlers to the area. One encounter occurred in the mid-1870s, when Susan Allison saw what she believed at first to be a huge tree trunk floating in the lake. A closer look, however, showed that it was a massive reptile swimming against the strong current. A mining superintendent named Thomas Smitheram saw the same sight from across the lake—though both he and Allison were ridiculed when they told what they had witnessed.

In 1900 a 10-year-old girl was terrified by a creature which surfaced and stared at her, approached much nearer, and stared more intently. The girl, who 70 years later said she still shivered as she recalled the incident, said she had been so frightened of the unknown creature that day that she ran indoors.

More recent descriptions of the monster of Lake Okanagan resemble the images in the Shushwap pictographs. The most noted feature in these recent descriptions involves the humps; witnesses describe a creature with three to five humps. In 1976 and again in 1977, Edward Fletcher of Vancouver said the Ogopogo swam near his boat with what he described as a flat, spiral motion. He said it looked "like a garter snake blown up to 70 or 75 feet."[57]

> **Did You Know?**
>
> Champ, the monster of Lake Champlain, has been sighted 194 times since 1982.

Champ of Lake Champlain

An equally terrifying lake monster appeared to Carl Roberts of Plattsburgh, New York, while fishing with two friends in June 2009.

The Earliest American Sea Monster?

A Jesuit missionary named Father Jacques Marquette was one of the first people ever to report a water monster in North American waters. Marquette, who accompanied French explorer Louis Joliet in his journey down the Mississippi River in 1673, was charged with keeping a journal detailing every step of their trip. The following entry is part of that journal:

> From time to time, we came upon monstrous fish, one of which struck the canoe with such violence that I thought it was a great tree about to break the canoe to pieces. On another occasion we saw on the water a MONSTER with the head of a tiger, a sharp nose like that of a wildcat with whiskers and straight, erect ears; the head was grey and the neck quite black; but we saw no more creatures of this sort.

Quoted in *Fate*, "An Early American Sea Monster," May 1984, p. 86.

The three men were casting off a dock on Lake Champlain, in upstate New York, when something caught Roberts's attention. It was evident that something was moving rapidly about 100 yards (91.4m) out in the water.

"It had to be 50 feet long, from what I could see of the humps," he told reporters the next morning. "There was no wind, no boats, no explanation whatsoever. It was so close that I could see the texture of the skin. It didn't move like a snake. It was not like a porpoise or a dolphin, either. It moved straight and fast, with its bumps up high and then down lower in the water."[58]

The creature is known as Champ, named for the lake in which it resides. It is the best known of the various mystery creatures that have been sighted in various lakes in the United States. Lake Champlain is massive, covering 436 square miles (1,129sq km)) along the borders of New York, Vermont, and Quebec. Champ (or its ancestors) has been sighted in Lake Champlain for centuries. Like Ogopogo, Champ was part of Indian legend—in this case, that of the Iroquois, who told frightening stories about a horned monster that lived in the lake. But it was Samuel de Champlain, a French explorer who gave the huge lake its name, whose sighting was the first documented one. In July 1609 he wrote that he was startled to see something that was "serpentlike," and "about 20 feet long, and thick as a barrel, with a head that resembled that of a horse."[59]

<aside>
Did You Know?

Monsters have been reported in 221 U.S. lakes, which is more than any other country, and lake monsters have been reported in 80 countries altogether.
</aside>

Area newspapers began covering sightings in the nineteenth century. In 1873 the *New York Times* reported on a railroad crew that was laying train tracks near Dresden, New York, when they saw the head of what they called "an enormous serpent" rise out of the water. Terrified, the men ran away. They later described the monster as having scales that glittered like silver. According to the article, "The appearance of his head was round and flat, with a hood spreading out from the lower part of it like a rubber cap often warn by mariners."[60]

A Picnic and a Monster

The most famous Champ sighting took place on July 5, 1977. Sandra and Anthony Mansi and her two young children were traveling through Vermont on rural route 36, when they stopped to have a picnic on the northeastern shore of Lake Champlain. After eating, the children played in the shallow water. As Sandra watched the children, she noticed a large object in the middle of the lake, approximately 150 feet (45.7m) away.

She first believed it was a large fish, but soon realized it was the head of a large creature coming to the surface of the lake. She later described it, as Samuel de Champlain had almost 400 years before, as looking like a serpent with a small, grayish brown head and a long snakelike neck. The head, she later recalled, was twisting around as though it were scanning the countryside. Frightened for her children, she called them out of the lake and ran back to the car to get her camera. She was able to get a picture before the monster submerged again.

Mansi's photograph, says zoologist Darren Nash, has caused quite a stir among cryptozoologists and amateur Champ watchers alike: "The Mansi photo has always been really popular because (unlike so many alleged lake monster photos) it's not too blurry or ambiguous, but clearly shows something that looks very much like a large, long-necked, grey aquatic animal. Rising from the water, it seems to be curving its neck over its rounded back, as if looking behind itself."[61]

> # Did You Know?
> In 1997 CNN sent a camera crew to Lake Van in Turkey, but they were unable to get any footage of the monster.

Authentic, with Reservations

The Mansi photograph and eyewitness account set off a flurry of discussion among cryptozoologists and other scientists. Several experts from the University of Chicago and the University of Arizona subjected the photograph to computer analysis and determined that it had not been doctored or touched up in any way.

In addition, experts meticulously studied the image of the monster, trying to determine whether it was indeed a living animal or some other object in the water. Both Roy Mackal of the University of Chicago and J. Richard Greenwell of the University of Arizona believed it was indeed an animal, probably related to one of two long-dead prehistoric species. Mackal speculated that it was descended from the zeuglodon, a primitive whale that was believed to have become extinct 20 million years ago. Greenwell, on the other hand, thought the animal could be related to the plesiosaur, as many believe the Loch Ness monster to be.

Others are not so sure. They point out, for example, that water can erode logs into unusual shapes, and they speculate that what the Mansis saw and photographed was just that—a partly submerged log. Others say that Lake Champlain is too shallow for a creature

The Giant Turtle of Hoan Kiem Lake

In the center of Hanoi, the capital of Vietnam, is Hoan Kiem Lake—the legendary home of a gigantic turtle that was said to have helped save the country from an invading army. According to the legend, in 1418 Emperor Le Loi called for help from the heavens in his effort to turn back the Chinese army. The answer to his prayer was a giant turtle that rose out of the lake and presented the emperor with a golden sword, which helped Le Loi triumph.

The story was believed to be merely a legend, for no turtles had been seen in the lake. However, in 1967 scientists at Hanoi National University were stunned to find the carcass of an enormous turtle washed up on the lake's shore. Its shell is estimated to be 40 inches (1m) across, and it weighs about 440 pounds (200kg). At more than 6 feet (1.9m) long, it matches the description of the legendary turtle. Other similar turtles have been seen only a few times since then. The turtle, say experts, is a good example of a giant cryptid that has been proven to really exist.

like a zeuglodon or a plesiosaur. To date, no one can say for sure what the Mansi family saw or what the photograph really shows.

As for Sandra Mansi, she found the whole experience an unhappy one. "I still have nightmares about the monster," she told researcher Loren Coleman. "The thing is chasing me, and I'm running to get away." But perhaps the worst part was the skepticism and ridicule she encountered after her story became public. "It's frightening," she said, "and sometimes I wish I hadn't told anyone about the picture, or I hadn't seen the monster."[62]

All Over the World

More lake monsters inhabit the world than the dozens reported to live in the lakes and rivers of North America. In fact, freshwater monsters have been spotted all over the world. One of the most interesting of these locations that many think is home to a dinosaur-like monster is Lake Van in Turkey, a huge, frigid body of water the size of Rhode Island.

Unlike many freshwater cryptids, the monster of Lake Van does not have a long history. No ancient legends about it are known, nor are there any reports of sightings that predate the 1990s. The monster first came to international attention in a newspaper article dated November 2, 1995. According to this article, a parliamentary commission had been assembled to form a search party to find out more about the monster that many witnesses—including the governor of the region—had seen firsthand.

More than 1,000 people who claim to have seen the monster describe it as being between 40 feet (12m) and 50 feet (15m) in length, with dark, mottled skin, two small eyes situated on top of its head, and sharp triangular humps on its back. Its head is shaped like that of a horse, and it has razor-sharp teeth that are very evident. Many of the eyewitnesses used the word "prehistoric" when describing it.

Not Just Serpents

Not every water monster resembles a serpent. Cryptozoologists say that some water monsters fit the description of mammals—warm-blooded vertebrates with hair or fur covering their skin, whose young are born alive and nourished with milk, and who cannot breathe underwater. Reports of one such water monster, described in witness accounts as a giant beaver, have come from parts of Canada and the United States. The average adult American beaver weighs 30 to 40 pounds (13.6kg to 18.1kg) and is 25 to 30 inches (63cm to 76cm) long, with an additional 9- to 10-inch-long tail (23cm to 25cm). According to witnesses, the Giant Beaver measures between 8 feet (2.5m) and 14 feet (4.2m) and weighs 450 to 600 pounds (204kg to 272kg). Like other beavers, the Giant Beaver is believed to spend 99 percent of its time in the water.

"It does sound like something from a science fiction film," admits cryptid researcher Madeline Mathes. "Giant animals do sound made-up, but really there are a number of them that were thought to be just legends, or even simply tall tales, but turn out to be real. Giant squids, for example, and giant sharks. Though witnesses have claimed to have seen them over the years, scientists were more than a little bit doubtful—but they were proved wrong."[63]

Like so many of the North American cryptids, the Giant Beaver is part of many Native American legends. The Pocumtuck people—who lived prior to 1800 in what is now Massachusetts—had a story about a large lake inhabited by a Giant Beaver. Though it mostly stayed in the water, according to the tale, it occasionally came ashore to hunt and kill humans. According to Deacon Phinehas Field, who collected and wrote down many of the stories of the Pocumtuck in the late nineteenth century, the Pocumtuck were eventually saved by a spirit they called Hobomock:

> The Great Beaver . . . made havoc among the fish and when these failed he would come ashore and devour Indians. A powwow was held and Hobomock raised, who came to their relief. With a great stake in hand, he waded the river until he found the beaver, and so hotly chased him that he sought to escape by digging into the ground. Hobomock saw his plan and his whereabouts, and with his great stake, jammed the beaver's head off. The earth over the beaver's head we call [the mountain] Sugarloaf, his body lies just to the north of it.[64]

Sightings and Fossils

The Giant Beaver might have remained simply a legend if one fossilized skeleton of the creature had not been found in the nineteenth century in Ohio and another in 1929 in central Illinois. The fossils proved the existence of giant beavers, which scientists gave the scientific name *Castoroides ohioensis*—Latin for "Beaver-like Creature of Ohio." However, scientists assumed that

these creatures, like many other prehistoric animals, lived about 2.6 million years ago and died out during the Ice Age more than 10,000 years ago.

But according to witnesses, Giant Beavers have shown up in several North American lakes in recent history—very much alive. In 1860 four young men reported seeing the Giant Beaver swimming in Bear Lake, Utah. They told the local newspaper that it was about 20 feet (6m) long and covered with "light brown fur like that of an otter."[65]

In 2009 Canadian researcher John Warms began touring areas in the United States and Canada where Giant Beaver sightings have been reported. Warms says that from what he has read, and the accounts of the people he has interviewed, he has no doubt that the creatures still reside in North American lakes. "I'm certain

The prehistoric Megalodon shark, depicted here attacking a whale, is believed to be the largest carnivore that ever lived. Fossil evidence suggests that Megalodon was more than 66 feet in length and weighed more than 100 tons.

they exist," he told the *Deseret News*. "I have encountered people in northern Manitoba and along the Alaskan Highways who claim to have seen the bear-sized creature. I saw one in southern Manitoba, swimming, and the head was about basketball size."[66]

A Remedy for Ridicule

Warms understands people's skepticism but stresses that the fear of being mocked keeps many witnesses from sharing their stories. He says that such reluctance is something that makes research difficult for all cryptozoologists. "I'm sure many more people must have seen [the Giant Beaver] around," he says, "but perhaps didn't want to be laughed at."[67]

The best antidote for ridicule, say experts, is finding data that can prove the existence of a water monster previously believed to be only legendary—whether that monster is a gigantic version of a known species or a cryptid not previously known. Though it is a difficult job—and one in which positive proof is never easy to find—such validation has occurred. And when it does, say cryptozoologists, that experience can completely change the way one looks at the natural world.

Chapter 5

On the Trail of Water Monsters

s intriguing as a detailed eyewitness account may be, especially when the eyewitness has a sterling reputation, that account is not proof of the existence of a water monster. For a scientist to add an animal to the catalog of creatures known to exist in the planet's rivers, lakes, or oceans, solid proof is an absolute necessity.

On the Trail of the Kraken

Though acquiring such proof sounds like a daunting job, scientists say it has been done before. Animals thought to be only the stuff of myth and legend—and even animals assumed to be extinct since prehistoric times—have been positively verified in modern times, surprising everyone. One good example is the giant squid.

Sixteenth-century Swedish archbishop and natural historian Olaus Magnus wrote down stories he had heard about an enormous squid known as the Kraken. Said to be the size of an island, the Kraken was feared by all sailors, for it could supposedly drag even the largest ships down to the bottom of the ocean. Some believe that the Scylla in *The Odyssey* was based on ancient stories about the Kraken. In 1869 Jules Verne wrote about a giant squid in his novel *Twenty Thousand Leagues Under the Sea*. Verne's book was science fiction; no one really believed that such a monster existed.

In the 1840s a French zoologist named Johan Japetus Steenstrup began looking into the legends of the Kraken. For years he had heard reports of carcasses of what appeared to be giant squid that had washed up on shore. Some of these accounts dated back to the seventeenth century. But while Steenstrup published scientific papers about the possibility of the giant squid being a reality, he had no solid evidence, and few of his peers took him seriously.

Eyes the Size of Soccer Balls

Steenstrup's interest in the giant cryptid was validated in a series of important steps. In 1853 he heard that fishermen had caught a huge squid and decided to cut it up into pieces and use it for bait. Steenstrup was able to get possession of the squid's beak and part of its throat, called the pharynx. He published a scientific paper in 1857 describing the parts of what he knew had to be the giant squid and gave the creature its Latin classification name, *Architeuthis*. Though his fellow scientists did not share his interest, two events soon captured their attention.

The first happened in 1873, when a man and his son found the carcass of a giant squid on a beach in Newfoundland. The two cut off one of its tentacles and showed it to a Canadian official, who estimated that the creature must have been at least 60 feet (18m) long. Seven years later, an entire carcass of a giant squid washed up on a beach in New Zealand, where local scientists documented it.

All over the world people heard about the finding of the entire body of a creature many had believed was only a myth. The average squid is less than 24 inches (60cm) long; this giant squid was 65 feet (19.8m) long. Its 40-foot-long tentacles (12m) and eight long arms were covered with spiked suction cups designed to catch and hold its prey. Most startling were its eyes, which were the size of soccer balls—the

Did You Know?

The word *kraken* comes from a Norse word for a stunted tree, because the creature was thought to look like a tree stump with its roots in the air.

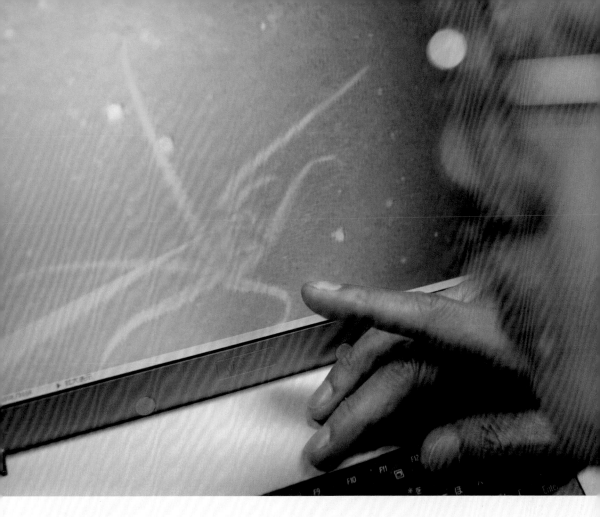

largest eyes in the animal kingdom, at least so far. The squid from New Zealand is still the largest one documented, but cryptozoologists Loren Coleman and Patrick Huyghe believe that much larger squid may exist: "Truly gigantic squids—much bigger than any found stranded yet—may survive in the deepest parts of the ocean, and may be only occasionally seen. Intriguingly, there are some eyewitness reports of squid being found as long as 90 feet (27.5m) in length."[68]

The first-known images of a giant squid were taken at about a 3,000 feet (900m) depth off the coast of Japan in 2004. A Japanese researcher shows one of the images on his computer. Though difficult to see, the squid is about 26 feet (8m) long.

Globsters and the Stronsay Beast

Dead giant squids that had washed ashore were helpful in finally verifying the creature's existence. However, such remains are not always so helpful. In many cases, a carcass is so decomposed that it

The Eyes Play Tricks

Roy Mackal is an authority on the Loch Ness monster and a founder of the International Society of Cryptozoology. He has always tempered his keen interest in cryptids with critical thinking. He once explained why witnesses to Nessie and other sea monsters are not always believable when they estimate size:

> You simply can never take anybody's estimate of size at face value, even if it's from a scientist. If you're looking over a body of water at some unknown animal, whether it's on the shore, or on the water, it's very difficult to estimate size. We cannot triangulate visually over a range of 20 feet. Over that range we estimate size by comparison, and if you're comparing an unknown animal to nothing else in the water, it's easy to be completely wrong. From the test we've run, we have found that even when we use objects whose size we know, people tend to be three to five times high in their estimates.

Quoted in Jerome Clark, "Interview with Dr. Roy Mackal: Tracking the Loch Ness Monsters," *Fate*, July 1977, pp. 38–39.

bears little resemblance to the animal it once was. In most cases, other animals or insects have chewed the remains.

Cryptozoologists call these enormous, unidentified carcasses "globsters"—a cross between "globs" and "monsters." But even the most enthusiastic believer in sea monsters acknowledges that globsters usually turn out to be something far less exotic than a sea monster.

One of the most famous globsters washed up on the rocks of Stronsay, one of the Orkney Islands off the coast of northern Scotland, in 1808. The badly decomposed carcass was 55 feet (16.7m) long, with a very small head on a 15-foot neck (4.5m), but because the tail was missing, scientists surmised that the beast must have been far longer. And because it was so strange and unfamiliar, naturalists from the Royal Museum in Edinburgh declared that the "Stronsay Beast" as it was dubbed, was a real sea monster.

However, modern scientists (including cryptozoologists) have expressed real doubts about the Stronsay Beast's true identity. Instead, they say that that particular globster was most likely a very large basking shark. The body of a basking shark decomposes in a particular way—with its jaw, gills, and characteristic triangular fin falling away. What remains looks nothing at all like a shark—and does resemble some prehistoric reptiles.

Sea Monsters and DNA

In recent years science has been able to take much of the guesswork out of globsters. More and more often, researchers can use DNA technology to identify mysterious remains. DNA is a complex

Fishermen unload a dead basking shark at a Portuguese port. As basking sharks decompose, the jaw, gills, and triangular fin fall away leaving remains that look more like a prehistoric reptile than a recently deceased shark.

chemical substance found in virtually every cell in an animal—including sea animals. It contains the genetic code passed down from parents to their offspring—nature's way of making sure that dogs give birth to dogs, horses to horses, and so on.

Scientists have ways to positively identify the DNA inside the cells taken from a human being or any other species from the animal kingdom. In the 1990s researchers began to store samples of DNA from known species of living things—from dandelions to giant sequoias, from red ants to killer whales. That DNA information is stored in a computerized library called the GenBank. That database has DNA information from more than 100,000 different species of plants and animals.

"The Hair's the Biggest Puzzle"

In August 2001 the GenBank came in very handy for researchers in Newfoundland, Canada. An enormous globster had washed ashore on Fortune Bay. The carcass was covered in coarse, white hair and was more than 18 feet (5.6m) long. No head was found, but a skeletal structure was visible, consisting of a large backbone and ribs.

The hair especially puzzled Ed Hodder, the fisherman who discovered it. "The hair's the biggest puzzle," he told interviewers. "What's hair doing on any kind of fish?"[69] Other residents agreed, saying it was very mysterious. Many of the residents were frightened, and even some of the veteran fishermen were uncomfortable just looking at it. Fisherman Tom Steward said it was like nothing he had ever seen in all his years on the sea. "We feel it's something strange," he said. "It's no ordinary thing."[70]

It turned out to be something very ordinary. Scientists took some of the flesh and extracted DNA from it. When they ran it through GenBank, the results showed that the DNA was that of a sperm whale. Much like the Stronsay Beast of 1808, this creature had decomposed in a way that made it unrecognizable to the experienced fishermen. What appeared to be hair on the carcass was actually the blubber, or inner fat, detaching from the body. When sperm whales decompose, their bodies take on a feathery, or hairy, look.

In this case, DNA proved the carcass was not that of a sea monster. Identifying "false" monsters is also part of a cryptozoologist's work, says Madeline Mathes. "Good cryptid researchers know that a lot of their work will prove fruitless as far as verifying a cryptid. Necessary work, yes, but definitely a lot less exciting."[71]

Sound Evidence

Sound technology is another tool that has proved to be especially promising for sea monster researchers. Back in the 1950s, the U.S. Navy's special underwater microphones, called hydrophones, were mounted on the ocean floor and connected to military communications centers on shore. That way, if an enemy submarine slipped into U.S. waters, the navy would know about it very quickly.

The supersensitive hydrophones found another use decades later. By placing the hydrophones in particular areas on the ocean floor, they could pick up the first creaks and cracks that precede a dangerous earthquake or tsunami. These modern hydrophone systems are manned by NOAA, the National Oceanic and Atmospheric Administration, and since the summer of 1997, something very odd has been happening. NOAA scientists have been hearing strange sounds from deep beneath the Pacific Ocean—sounds unlike anything they have ever heard before. And many wonder whether the noises could be coming from sea monsters.

> **Did You Know?**
> About 4,000 sightings of the Loch Ness Monster have been reported, according to the BBC's Nicholas Witchell.

Christopher Fox is a NOAA scientist who believes some of these mysterious noises are the sounds of gigantic cryptids. Fox says that he and his fellow scientists hear sounds from the depths all the time, and they are very good at identifying the sources while looking at the sound waves on their high-tech equipment. "Sound waves are almost like voice prints," he explains. "You're able to look at the characteristics of the sound and say, 'There's a blue whale, there's a fin whale, there's a boat, there's a humpback whale, and here comes an earthquake.'"[72]

But the sound first heard in 1997 was unidentifiable. It was definitely a living thing rather than a boat or the rumbling of an earthquake. It was extremely loud—so loud, in fact, that it was picked up by several of the hydrophones covering an area of 3,100 square miles (4,800km). The volume of this noise, say experts, was far greater than the sound made by any animal known to science. The NOAA scientists named the mystery sound Bloop, because when they speeded the noise up to see if they could detect more information, it sounded a bit like bubbles. For now, Bloop seems as good a name as any until researchers can finally identify the source of that monstrous sound and give it a more dignified-sounding Latin classification name.

Side-Scan Sonar

Meanwhile, some cryptid researchers have been using technology that enables them to go where the sea or lake monsters are likely to be. Instead of waiting for one of the creatures to surface and hope that someone with a good camera is standing by, they are using tools, such as side-scan sonar, that can help them "see"—even in the deepest, murkiest water.

The torpedo-shaped side-scan sonar unit is about four feet (1.2m) long. It is dragged behind a boat, and as it moves, it sends out pulses of sound waves, called "pings," in a 180-degree arc. As the pings bounce off solid objects under the water, they return to the sonar unit, which feeds them into a computer. The computer can turn those pings into an image of whatever objects are on the lake or ocean bottom.

Rescuers use side-scan sonar to find submerged boats and ships, and bodies that may still be lying on the bottom. And some researchers have found that side-scan sonar can provide images of creatures

> **Did You Know?**
>
> A fish called the coelacanth, believed to have become extinct 65 million years ago, was found in a fish market in South Africa in 1938.

Police use side-scan sonar units such as this one to search bodies of water for missing people. Cryptid researchers also use these units to search beneath lakes and seas for water monsters.

moving along the lake or ocean floor, too—in some cases, too large to be fish or any other known animal.

Finding Selma

Jan Sundberg is a cryptozoologist who claims he has used side-scan sonar, together with portable hydrophones, with some success. Sundberg has spent a great deal of time trying to verify the existence of

The Ridicule Factor

One researcher, author June O'Neill, gives a good example of how the fear of being laughed at is depriving crypto-zoologists of important data about sea serpents. She says:

> A good friend of mine who is a Lieutenant in the U.S. Coast Guard saw, in the company of several other officers, an unknown creature in the mid-Atlantic while on a U.S. Coast Guard ship in the mid-1990s. From the bridge it appeared to be brownish in color and about 50 feet long. It circled their ship for about 15 to 20 minutes at a relatively rapid pace. At no time did it 'blow,' nor did it have any observable dorsal (back) or caudal (tail) fin, ruling out sharks or whales. They did not see a head or neck. All on the bridge asked what it was and none had ever seen anything like it, but they did not call it a "Sea Serpent" or "Sea Monster." It was not officially logged.

Quoted in Loren Coleman and Patrick Huyghe, *The Field Guide to Lake Monsters, Sea Serpents, and Other Mystery Denizens of the Deep.* New York: Jeremy P. Tarcher/Penguin, 2003, p. 274.

Selma, a monster said to lurk in Lake Seljord, in southern Norway. Sightings of Selma go back to the eighteenth century, when a handful of witnesses reported seeing a 30-foot-long (9m), eel-like creature with the head of a horse or an elk. Like many water monsters, Selma has eluded researchers.

In 2005, however, Sundberg told a Norwegian television station that he and his team had found something exciting: "I have news today. . . . Between noon and 2 P.M. we got two large objects on sonar; they were four to five meters long and this was no fish. Afterwards we heard some very loud noises on the hydrophone. The sounds were so powerful that our headphones banged and vibrated."[73]

Though Sundberg and his team were not able to determine what was creating the loud sounds on their hydrophone, five years afterward they remain convinced that it was Selma—or a sea monster equally large. Sundberg also is certain that it is only a matter of time until teams like his will prove the creature's existence. "The search for Selma the Sea Serpent will continue," he told reporters in March 2010, "and we're getting closer each summer to proving beyond a reasonable doubt that she's here."[74]

A British Royal Air Force bomber that crashed in Loch Ness is visible in this sonar image. The side-scan sonar unit sends out pulses of sound waves that bounce off solid objects underwater. That information is then fed into a computer, which creates an image.

"Nothing Can Take That Away"

Despite some success stories in showing the possible existence of sea monsters, many people still consider them more fiction than fact. Those who doubt that sea monsters exist do have some data on their side. For example, in 2003 the BBC sponsored a thorough search of Loch Ness using satellite tracking devices and 600 individual sonar units. Although earlier attempts had found unusual underwater shapes using sonar, the BBC project found no living thing larger than a fish in the lake. As a result, many people no longer think that Nessie is real.

For others, however, even those who were dubious about such monsters, the experience of actually seeing one has proven to be a life-changing experience—no matter what the latest study may show. Robert Rines, a physics expert, said he caught a glimpse of Nessie in 1971 while visiting the lake with his wife and two friends. Until his death in 2009, Rines devoted himself to searching for the monster. "It looked like the back of an elephant," he later told a reporter from the *Boston Globe*. "I know there was a big unknown thing in that lake. That's why I haven't let go."[75]

> ## Did You Know?
> Researcher Robert Rines once hired a perfume maker to concoct a scent that he hoped would attract the Loch Ness monster.

Rines did not worry about what other people thought of him. He felt the search was worthwhile: "There are a few of us willing to risk our reputations on something as improbable as this, judged with such ridicule. Scientists think there are other things to do for fame and fortune than something this crazy. So we do it quietly as a private venture, and don't have to hear that we're crazy people chasing monsters."[76]

Ian Cameron, the retired police supervisor who witnessed what he is certain was the Loch Ness monster years ago, would agree. He has never changed his mind about what he saw, no matter what studies say. "I saw it," he says simply, "and nothing can take that away."[77]

Source Notes

Introduction: Monsters Among Us?

1. Quoted in Loren Coleman, "South Africa: New Mermaid Sighting," *Cryptomundo*, January 16, 2008. www.cryptomundo.com.
2. Quoted in Coleman, "South Africa: New Mermaid Sighting."
3. Quoted in *NOVA*, "The Beast of Loch Ness," PBS, January 12, 1999. www.pbs.org.
4. Quoted in *NOVA*, "The Beast of Loch Ness."
5. Quoted in Loren Coleman and Patrick Huyghe, *The Field Guide to Lake Monsters and Sea Serpents*. New York: Jeremy P. Tarcher/Penguin, 2003, p. 95.
6. Quoted in Coleman and Huyghe, *The Field Guide*, p. 95.

Chapter One: From the Ocean's Depths

7. Homer, *The Odyssey*, Great Literature Online. http://homer.classic authors.net.
8. Homer, *The Odyssey*.
9. Quoted in Jeffrey Cooley, "A Star Is Born: Mesopotamian and Classical Catasterisms," *Humanitas*, Fall 2006, p. 11.
10. Quoted in Richard Heidel, *The Babylonian Genesis: The Story of Creation*. Chicago: University of Chicago Press, 1951, p. 143.
11. Quoted in Unknown Explorers, "Sea Serpents." www.unknownexplorers. com.
12. Quoted in W. Ritchie Benedict, "Sea Serpents—an Endangered Species or Totally Extinct?" *Fate*, November 2004, p. 68.
13. Quoted in Benedict, "Sea Serpents," p. 68.
14. Quoted in Richard Ellis, *Monsters of the Sea*. New York: Alfred A. Knopf, 1994, pp. 49–50.
15. Quoted in American Monsters, "Gloucester Sea Serpent." http://american monsters.com.

16. Quoted in Ellis, *Monsters of the Sea*, p. 59.
17. Quoted in Matthew A. Bille, "The Definitive Sea Serpent," *Strange Magazine*. www.strangemag.com.
18. Quoted in Bille, "The Definitive Sea Serpent."
19. Quoted in Bille, "The Definitive Sea Serpent."
20. Benedict, "Sea Serpents," p. 74.
21. Quoted in Centre Culturel Marie-Anne-Gaboury, "Canada's Lake Creature." http://cnc.virtuelle.ca.
22. Quoted in "Canada's Lake Creature."
23. Quoted in Benedict, "Sea Serpents," p. 74.
24. Quoted in Benedict, "Sea Serpents," p. 74.
25. Quoted in Coleman and Huyghe, *The Field Guide*, p. 102.
26. Quoted in Scott Corrales, "Our Haunted Seas," *Fate*, November 2005, p. 54.
27. Quoted in Corrales, "Our Haunted Seas," p. 54.

Chapter Two: Mer-People

28. Quoted in Gary R. Varner, *Creatures in the Mist: Little People, Wild Men, and Spirit Beings Around the World*. New York: Algora, 2007, p. 13.
29. Pausanias, *Description of Greece*, trans. J.G. Frazer. Internet Archive. www.archive.org.
30. E. Randall Floyd, *Great Southern Mysteries*. Little Rock, AR: August House, 1989, p. 119.
31. Floyd, *Great Southern Mysteries*, p. 118.
32. Floyd, *Great Southern Mysteries*, p. 119.
33. Otha Barhma, "Adventure on the Singing River," *Meridian (MS) Star*, April 26, 2007. http://meridianstar.com.
34. Christopher Columbus, "January 9, 1493," *The Diary of Christopher Columbus*, Northstar Gallery.com. http://northstargallery.com.
35. Quoted in Ellis, *Monsters of the Sea*, p. 79.
36. Quoted in Geoffrey Fox, "Mermaids and Other Fetishes," Scribd. www.scribd.com.
37. George M. Eberhart, *Mysterious Creatures: A Guide to Cryptozoology*. Santa Barbara, CA: ABC-CLIO, 2002, p. 331.

38. Quoted in Ellis, *Monsters of the Sea*, p. 82.

39. Michael A. Souza, "Japan's Mermaids," *Fate*, May 2004, pp. 69–70.

40. Quoted in *Israel Hayom*, "'Mermaid' Spotted on Kiryat Yam Beach," Arutz Sheva, August 12, 2009. www.israelnationalnews.com.

Chapter Three: The Monster in Loch Ness

41. Quoted in Scotland's Culture, "Loch Ness Sightings." www.ltscotland.org.uk.

42. Quoted in "Loch Ness Sightings."

43. Quoted in "Loch Ness Sightings."

44. Quoted in Rupert Gould, *The Loch Ness Monster and Others*. New York: University Books, 1969, p. 28.

45. Dolores Ann Griffith, telephone interview with the author, April 17, 2010.

46. Quoted in *NOVA*, "The Beast of Loch Ness."

47. Quoted in Gould, *The Loch Ness Monster and Others*, p. 44.

48. Quoted in On This Day: 1950–2005, "1987: Search Ends for Loch Ness Monster," BBC Home. http://news.bbc.co.uk.

49. Quoted in Ellis, *Monsters of the Sea*, p. 23.

50. Quoted in Ellis, *Monsters of the Sea*, p. 25.

51. Madeline Mathes, telephone interview with the author, May 1, 2010.

52. Mathes, telephone interview.

53. Quoted in Coleman and Huyghe, *The Field Guide to Lake Monsters*, p. 21.

54. Quoted in Coleman and Huyghe, *The Field Guide to Lake Monsters*, p. 21.

55. Quoted in *NOVA*, "The Beast of Loch Ness."

Chapter Four: Beasts in the Lakes

56. Mary Moon, "Ogopogo: Canada's Loch Ness Monster," *Fate*, November 1978, p. 34.

57. Quoted in Moon, "Ogopogo," p. 38.

58. Quoted in Cryptomundo, "New Champ Sighting: Wilcox Dock Incident." http://cryptomundo.com.

59. Quoted in Jerome Clark, "America's New Water Monsters: The New Evidence," *Fate*, April 1983, p. 63.

60. Quoted in Museum of Unnatural History, "Champ of Lake Champlain." http://www.unmuseum.org.

61. Quoted in Tetrapod Zoology, "Best Lake Monster Image Ever." http://scienceblogs.com.

62. Quoted in Coleman and Huyghes, *The Field Guide to Lake Monsters*, p. 115.

63. Mathes, telephone interview.

64. Quoted in Absolute Astronomy, "Potumtuck Range." www.absoluteastronomy.com.

65. Quoted in Coleman and Huyghe, *The Field Guide to Lake Monsters*, p. 195.

66. Quoted in Lynn Arave, "Canadian in Utah to Seek 'Strange Creatures Seldom Seen,'" *Deseret News*. www.deseretnews.com.

67. Quoted in Arave, "Canadian in Utah to Seek 'Strange Creatures Seldom Seen.'"

Chapter Five: On the Trail of Water Monsters

68. Coleman and Huyge, *The Field Guide to Lake Monsters*, p. 7.

69. Quoted in 21st Century Radio, "Unknown Sea 'Monster' Washes Ashore in Newfoundland." www.21stcenturyradio.com.

70. Quoted in 21st Century Radio, "Unknown Sea 'Monster' Washes Ashore in Newfoundland."

71. Mathes, telephone interview.

72. Quoted in Micah A. Hanks, "Apocalypse at Sea," *Fate*, March 2007, p. 12.

73. Quoted in Jonathan Tisdall, "New Sea Serpent Claim," *Aftenposten* (Norway). www.aftenposten.no.

74. Quoted in American Monster, "Jan-Ove Sundberg Interview," March 17, 2010. http://americanmonster.com.

75. Quoted in Cryptomundo, "Loch Ness Hero Robert Rines Dies," November 2, 2009. www.cryptomundo.com.

76. Quoted in Cryptomundo, "Loch Ness Hero Robert Rines Dies."

77. Quoted in *NOVA*, "The Beast of Loch Ness."

For Further Exploration

Books

Rick Emmer, *The Loch Ness Monster: Fact or Fiction?* New York: Chelsea House, 2010.

Mike Everhart, *Sea Monsters: Prehistoric Creatures of the Deep.* Washington, DC: National Geographic, 2007.

Dale Jarvis, *Wonderful Strange: Ghosts, Fairies, and Fabulous Beasties.* St. John's, Newfoundland, Canada: Flanker, 2005.

Stuart A. Kallen, *The Loch Ness Monster.* San Diego, CA: ReferencePoint, 2009.

Mary Pope Osborne and Natalie Pope Boyce, *Sea Monsters.* New York: Random House, 2008.

Gary R. Varner, *Creatures in the Mist: Little People, Wild Men and Spirit Beings Around the World.* New York: Algora, 2007.

Web Sites

Champ of Lake Champlain (http://unmuseum.mus.pa.us/champ.html). This is a helpful Web site that goes through the history of the monster and what possibilities could explain it. It contains links to other sea monsters, too—including Loch Ness and the Kraken.

Cryptomundo: It's a Cryptid World (www.cryptomundo.com/cryptozoo-news). Cryptozoologists such as noted author Loren Coleman provide information on the history, sightings, and latest research on cryptids, both land and water creatures. There are also biographies of some of the pioneers of cryptozoology.

The Legend of Nessie: The Ultimate Loch Ness Monster Site (www.nessie.co.uk). One of the most up-to-date of the sea monster Web sites, this one has information on some of the most recent sightings, as well as footage and photos shot of Nessie. Excellent link to the Nessie hunters.

NOAA's Vents Program: Acoustic Monitoring (www.pmel.noaa.gov/vents/acoustics/spectrograms.html). This site shows visual images and audio of sounds recorded in the oceans. Readers can see the difference between spectrograms showing the frequencies of whales and dolphins, ships, seismic noises, and Bloop, as well as hear their very different sounds. There is also helpful information on how these noises are monitored.

NOVA: **The Beast of Loch Ness** (www.pbs.org/wgbh/nova/lochness). This site contains eyewitness interviews, historic references to Nessie, and information about the ways that cryptozoologists are trying to discover whether there really is a monster in Loch Ness.

Ogopogo Quest (www.ogopogoquest.com). Legends, history, methods of searching, and an introduction to some of the cryptozoologists who are trying to prove Ogopogo's existence are all included on this site.

StrangeArk (www.strangeark.com). One of the most fascinating sites dealing with cryptids. The archives section contains dozens of descriptions of interesting animals recently discovered throughout the world, as well as creatures still classified as cryptids.

Index

Picture Credits

About the Author

Gail B. Stewart has written more than 260 books for teens and young adults. She is the mother of three grown sons and lives with her husband in Minneapolis, Minnesota.